973   34880000462387
Tra   BOOK CHARGING CARD 18.37
C.1   Accession No. _____ Call No. dup
Author Travis, George
Title State Facts

Date Loaned	Borrower's Name	Date Returned

Bound to Stay Bound Books, Inc.

The Rourke Guide
to State Symbols

STATE FACTS

George Travis

The Rourke Press, Inc.
Vero Beach, Florida 32964

PHOTO CREDITS: Cover courtesy of Corel

COVER ILLUSTRATION: Jim Spence

CREATIVE SERVICES:
East Coast Studios, Merritt Island, Florida

EDITORIAL SERVICES:
Janice L. Smith for Penworthy

Library of Congress Cataloging-in-Publication Data

Travis, George, 1961-
   State facts / George Travis.
     p. cm. — (The Rourke guide to state symbols)
   Includes index.
   Summary: A compilation of information on the nicknames, land area, coastline, temperatures, precipitation, and more for each of the fifty states.
   ISBN 1-57103-297-5
   1. U.S. states Miscellanea Juvenile literature. 2. United States Miscellanea Juvenile literature. [1. United States Miscellanea.] I. Title. II. Series.
E180.T73 1999
973—dc21
                                             99-31454
                                               CIP

Printed in the USA

Table of Contents

INTRODUCTION

The size and shape of each of the 50 states has changed little over the past hundred years. From our smallest state, Rhode Island, to our largest state, Alaska, our borders create one of the most diverse and dynamic countries in the world.

Geologically, the states have continued to change. Valleys have become deeper and mountains higher. In Hawaii, the 50th state, Mauna Kea is the tallest peak. It is a dormant volcano which started on the ocean floor and grew to 31,796 feet. When it erupts again it could grow even higher.

Changes to the United States will continue to occur. Coastlines will change as ocean waves erode away at the land. Population growth and other influences may cause borders to someday change again as the United States of America continues to evolve.

Note: The coastline mileage referenced in this book is ocean coastline only.

ALABAMA

Means "Tribal Town" in Creek Indian language

Nicknames: Heart of Dixie, Cotton State or Yellowhammer State

Statehood: December 14, 1819

Population: 4,304,400; Rank: 23rd

Capital: Montgomery

Largest City: Birmingham

Land Area: 50,766 square miles; Rank: 28th

Number of Counties: 67

Highest Point: Cheaha Mountain: 2,407 feet

Coastline: 53 miles

Inland Water: 938 square miles

Bordering States: Florida, Georgia, Mississippi, Tennessee

ALASKA

Based on Eskimo word "Alakshak"
meaning "Great Lands" or "Peninsula"

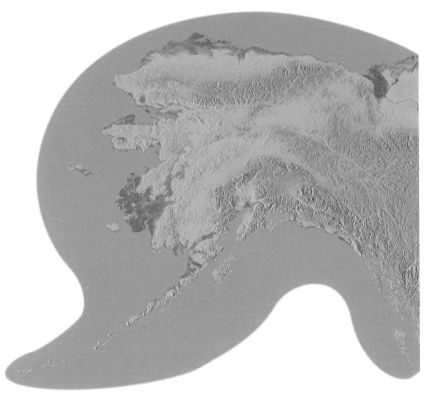

Nicknames: Last Frontier, Great Land or Land of the Midnight Sun

Statehood: January 3, 1959

Population: 609,200; Rank: 48th

Capital: Juneau

Largest City: Anchorage

Land Area: 570,833 square miles; Rank: 1st

Number of Counties: 25

Highest Point: Mt. McKinley: 20,320 feet

Coastline: 5,580 miles

Inland Water: 20,171 square miles

Bordering States: None

ARIZONA

Spanish interpretation of "Arizuma," an Aztec Indian word meaning "Silver-Bearing;" also based on Pima Indian word "Arizonac" meaning "Little Spring Place."

Nickname: Grand Canyon State
Statehood: February 14, 1912
Population: 4,513,500; Rank: 21st
Capital: Phoenix
Largest City: Phoenix
Land Area: 113,510 square miles; Rank: 6th
Number of Counties: 15
Highest Point: Humphrey Peak: 12,633 feet
Coastline: 0 miles
Inland Water: 492 square miles
Bordering States: California, Colorado, Nevada, New Mexico, Utah

ARKANSAS

French interpretation of the Sioux word "Acansa,"
meaning "Downstream Place."

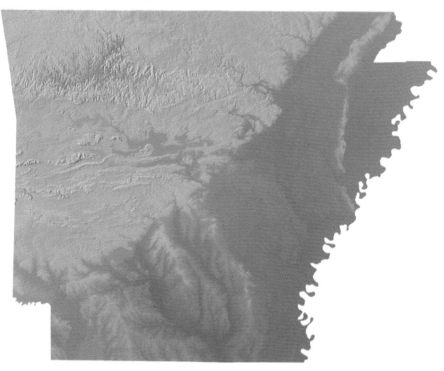

Nicknames: The Natural State, Land of Opportunity
or Wonder State
Statehood: June 15, 1836
Population: 2,527,600; Rank: 33rd
Capital: Little Rock
Largest City: Little Rock
Land Area: 52,082 square miles; Rank: 27th
Number of Counties: 75
Highest Point: Magazine Mountain: 2,753 feet
Coastline: 0 miles
Inland Water: 1,109 square miles
Bordering States: Louisiana, Mississippi, Missouri, Oklahoma,
Tennessee, Texas

CALIFORNIA

*Named after Califia, a mythical paradise
in a Spanish romance written by Montalvo in 1510*

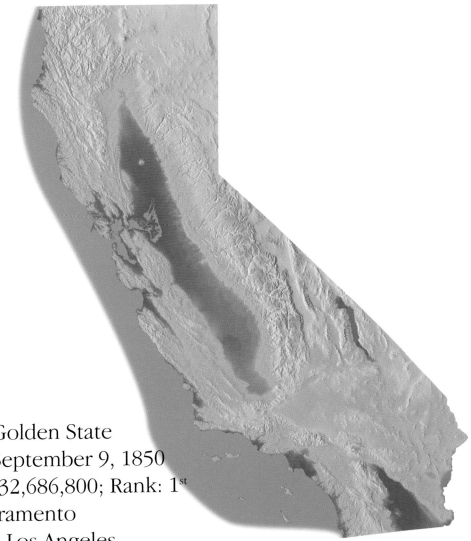

Nickname: Golden State
Statehood: September 9, 1850
Population: 32,686,800; Rank: 1st
Capital: Sacramento
Largest City: Los Angeles
Land Area: 156,297 square miles; Rank: 3rd
Number of Counties: 58
Highest Point: Mt. Whitney: 14,494 feet
Coastline: 840 miles
Inland Water: 2,407 square miles
Bordering States: Arizona, Nevada, Oregon

COLORADO

*Taken from the Spanish word for the color red,
which was applied to the Colorado River*

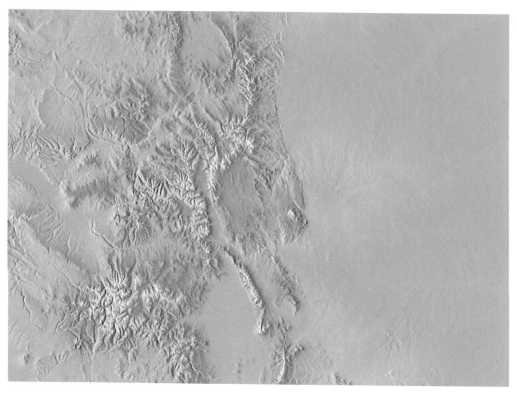

Nickname: Centennial State
Statehood: August 1, 1876
Population: 3,849,400; Rank: 25th
Capital: Denver
Largest City: Denver
Land Area: 103,598 square miles; Rank: 8th
Number of Counties: 63
Highest Point: Mt. Elbert: 14,433 feet
Coastline: 0 miles
Inland Water: 496 square miles
Bordering States: Arizona, Kansas, Nebraska, New Mexico,
Oklahoma, Utah, Wyoming

CONNECTICUT

*Based on Mohican and Algonquin Indian words
for "Place Beside a Long River."*

Nicknames: Constitution State, Provision State or Nutmeg State
Statehood: January 9, 1788
Population: 3,280,100; Rank: 28th
Capital: Hartford
Largest City: Bridgeport
Land Area: 4,872 square miles; Rank: 48th
Number of Counties: 8
Highest Point: Mt. Frissell: 2,380 feet
Coastline: 0 miles
Inland Water: 147 square miles
Bordering States: Massachusetts, New York, Rhode Island

DELAWARE

Named after Lord De La Warr, an early governor of Virginia

Nicknames: First State or Diamond State
Statehood: December 7, 1787
Population: 731,900; Rank: 46th
Capital: Dover
Largest City: Wilmington
Land Area: 1,933 square miles; Rank: 49th
Number of Counties: 3
Highest Point: Ebright Azimuth: 442 feet
Coastline: 28 miles
Inland Water: 112 square miles
Bordering States: Maryland, New Jersey, Pennsylvania

FLORIDA

Named Pascua Florida, meaning "Flowery Easter," on Easter 1513 by Spanish explorer Ponce de Leon

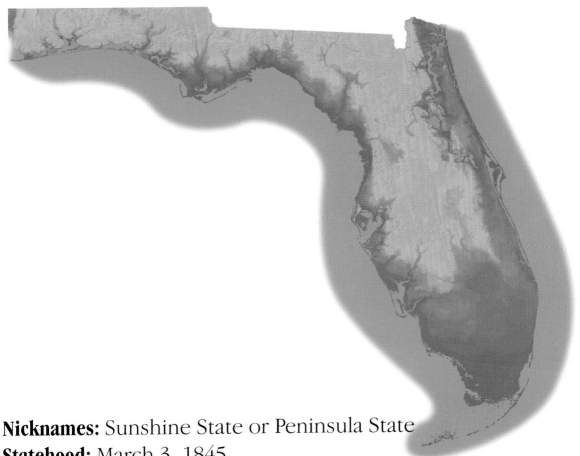

Nicknames: Sunshine State or Peninsula State

Statehood: March 3, 1845

Population: 14,701,200; Rank: 4th

Capital: Tallahassee

Largest City: Jacksonville

Land Area: 54,157 square miles; Rank: 26th

Number of Counties: 67

Highest Point: Britton Hill: 345 feet

Coastline: 1,350 miles

Inland Water: 4,511 square miles

Bordering States: Alabama, Georgia

GEORGIA

Named for King George II of England

Nicknames: Peach State, Goober State or Empire of the South
Statehood: January 2, 1788
Population: 7,421,800; Rank: 10th
Capital: Atlanta
Largest City: Atlanta
Land Area: 58,060 square miles; Rank: 21st
Number of Counties: 159
Highest Point: Brasstown Bald: 4,784 feet
Coastline: 100 miles
Inland Water: 854 square miles
Bordering States: Alabama, Florida, North Carolina, South Carolina, Tennessee

HAWAII

Based on "Owhyhee," the native Hawaiian word for "homeland"

Nicknames: Aloha State or Paradise of the Pacific
Statehood: August 21, 1959
Population: 1,185,800; Rank: 41st
Capital: Honolulu
Largest City: Honolulu
Land Area: 6,427 square miles; Rank:47th
Number of Counties: 5
Highest Point: Mauna Kea: 13,796 feet
Coastline: 750 miles
Inland Water: 46 square miles
Bordering States: None

IDAHO

A coined, or invented word, supposedly meaning "Gem of the Mountains"

Nickname: Gem State
Statehood: July 3, 1890
Population: 1,200,800; Rank: 40th
Capital: Boise
Largest City: Boise
Land Area: 82,413 square miles; Rank: 11th
Number of Counties: 44
Highest Point: Borah Peak: 12,662 feet
Coastline: 0 miles
Inland Water: 1,153 square miles
Bordering States: Montana, Nevada, Oregon, Utah, Washington, Wyoming

ILLINOIS

Based on the Algonquin Indian word for "Warriors"

Nicknames: Land of Lincoln or Prairie State
Statehood: December 3, 1818
Population: 11,931,700; Rank: 6th
Capital: Springfield
Largest City: Chicago
Land Area: 55,646 square miles; Rank: 24th
Number of Counties: 120
Highest Point: Charles Mound: 1,235 feet
Coastline: 0 miles
Inland Water: 700 square miles
Bordering States: Indiana, Iowa, Kentucky, Missouri, Wisconsin

INDIANA

A word meaning "Land of the Indians"

Nickname: Hoosier State
Statehood: December 11, 1816
Population: 5,864,000; Rank: 14th
Capital: Indianapolis
Largest City: Indianapolis
Land Area: 35,936 square miles; Rank: 38th
Number of Counties: 92
Highest Point: Hoosier Hill: 1,257 feet
Coastline: 0 mile
Inland Water: 253 square miles
Bordering States: Illinois, Kentucky, Michigan, Ohio

IOWA

Nickname: Hawkeye State or Corn State
Statehood: December 28, 1846
Population: 2,869,413; Rank: 30th
Capital: Des Moines
Largest City: Des Moines
Land Area: 55,965 square miles; Rank: 23rd
Number of Counties: 99
Highest Point: High Point: 1,670 feet
Coastline: 0 miles
Inland Water: 310 square miles
Bordering States: Illinois, Minnesota, Missouri, Nebraska, South Dakota, Wisconsin

KANSAS

From the Sioux Indian word for "South Wind People"

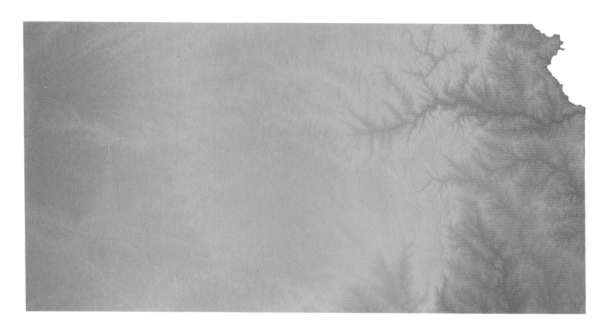

Nickname: Sunflower State
Statehood: January 29, 1861
Population: 2,585,800; Rank: 32nd
Capital: Topeka
Largest City: Wichita
Land Area: 81,783 square miles; Rank: 13th
Number of Counties: 105
Highest Point: Mt. Sunflower: 4,039 feet
Coastline: 0 miles
Inland Water: 499 square miles
Bordering States: Colorado, Missouri, Nebraska, Oklahoma

KENTUCKY

*Based on the Iroquois Indian word
"Ken-tah-ten" meaning "Land of Tomorrow."*

Nickname: Bluegrass State
Statehood: June 1, 1792
Population: 3,896,900; Rank: 24th
Capital: Frankfort
Largest City: Louisville
Land Area: 39,674 square miles; Rank: 36th
Number of Counties: 120
Highest Point: Black Mountain: 4,145 feet
Coastline: 0 miles
Inland Water: 740 square miles
Bordering States: Illinois, Indiana, Missouri, Ohio, Tennessee, Virginia, West Virginia

LOUISIANA

Named in honor of France's King Louis XIV

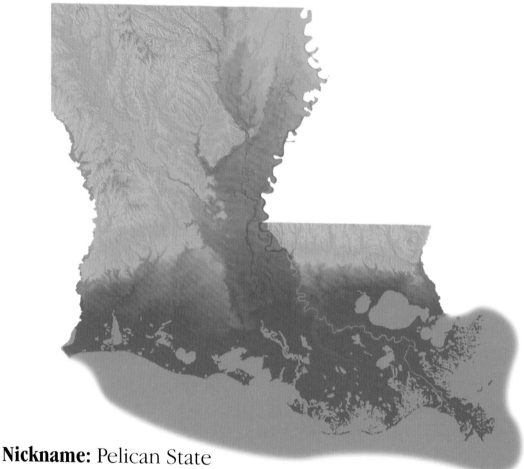

Nickname: Pelican State
Statehood: April 30, 1812
Population: 4,358,200; Rank: 22nd
Capital: Baton Rouge
Largest City: New Orleans
Land Area: 44,520 square miles; Rank: 33rd
Number of Counties: 64
Highest Point: Driskill Mountain: 535 feet
Coastline: 397 miles
Inland Water: 3,230 square miles
Bordering States: Arkansas, Mississippi, Texas

MAINE

Assumed to be a reference to the state region being a mainland, different from its many surrounding islands

Nickname: Pine Tree State

Statehood: March 15, 1820

Population: 1,241,300; Rank: 39th

Capital: Augusta

Largest City: Portland

Land Area: 30,995 square miles; Rank: 39th

Number of Counties: 16

Highest Point: Katahdin Mountain: 5,268 feet

Coastline: 228 miles

Inland Water: 2,270 square miles

Bordering States: New Hampshire

MARYLAND

Named in honor of Henrietta Maria, wife of England's King Charles I

Nickname: Old Line State

Statehood: April 28, 1788

Population: 5,068,300; Rank: 19th

Capital: Annapolis

Largest City: Baltimore

Land Area: 9,838 square miles; Rank: 42nd

Number of Counties: 23

Highest Point: Backbone Mountain: 3,360 feet

Coastline: 31 miles

Inland Water: 623 square miles

Bordering States: Delaware, Pennsylvania, Virginia, West Virginia

MASSACHUSETTS

Named after a local Indian tribe whose name means "A Large Hill Place"

Nickname: Bay State
Statehood: February 6, 1788
Population: 6,115,300; Rank: 13th
Capital: Boston
Largest City: Boston
Land Area: 7,826 square miles; Rank: 45th
Number of Counties: 14
Highest Point: Mt. Greylock: 3,491 feet
Coastline: 192 miles
Inland Water: 460 square miles
Bordering States: Connecticut, New Hampshire, New York, Rhode Island, Vermont

MICHIGAN

From the Chippewa Indian word "Meicigama," meaning "Great Water"

Nicknames: Great Lakes State, Wolverine State or Water Wonderland

Statehood: January 26, 1837

Population: 9,632,100; Rank: 8th

Capital: Lansing

Largest City: Detroit

Land Area: 56,959 square miles; Rank: 22nd

Number of Counties: 83

Highest Point: Mt. Arvon: 1,980 feet

Coastline: 0 miles

Inland Water: 1,573 square miles

Bordering States: Indiana, Ohio, Wisconsin

MINNESOTA

Based on the Dakota Sioux Indian word for "Sky-tinted Water," referring to the Minnesota River

Nicknames: North Star State, Gopher State, or Bread & Butter State

Statehood: May 11, 1858

Population: 4,683,800; Rank: 20th

Capital: St. Paul

Largest City: Minneapolis

Land Area: 79,548 square miles; Rank: 14th

Number of Counties: 87

Highest Point: Eagle Mountain: 2,301 feet

Coastline: 0 miles

Inland Water: 4,854 square miles

Bordering States: Iowa, North Dakota, South Dakota, Wisconsin

MISSISSIPPI

Possibly based on Chippewa Indian words
"Mici Zibi," loosely translated as "Great River"

Nickname: Magnolia State
Statehood: December 10, 1817
Population: 2,719,100; Rank: 31st
Capital: Jackson
Largest City: Jackson
Land Area: 47,234 square miles; Rank: 31st
Number of Counties: 82
Highest Point: Woodall Mountain: 806 feet
Coastline: 53 miles
Inland Water: 938 square miles
Bordering States: Alabama, Arkansas, Louisiana, Tennessee

MISSOURI

Named after Missouri Indian tribe whose name means "Town of the Large Canoes"

Nickname: Show-Me State
Statehood: August 10, 1821
Population: 5,380,500; Rank: 16th
Capital: Jefferson City
Largest City: Kansas City
Land Area: 68,946 square miles; Rank: 18th
Number of Counties: 114
Highest Point: Taum Sauk Mountain: 1,772 feet
Coastline: 0 miles
Inland Water: 752 square miles
Bordering States: Arkansas, Illinois, Iowa, Kansas, Kentucky, Nebraska, Oklahoma, Tennessee

MONTANA

Based on the Spanish word for "Mountainous"

Nickname: Treasure State
Statehood: November 8, 1889
Population: 884,300; Rank: 44th
Capital: Helena
Largest City: Billings
Land Area: 145,388 square miles; Rank: 4th
Number of Counties: 56
Highest Point: Granite Peak: 12,799 feet
Coastline: 0 miles
Inland Water: 1,657 square miles
Bordering States: Idaho, North Dakota, South Dakota, Wyoming

NEBRASKA

Based on an Oto Indian word that means "Flat Water," referring to the Platte River

Nickname: Cornhusker State
Statehood: March 1, 1867
Population: 1,664,200; Rank: 38th
Capital: Lincoln
Largest City: Omaha
Land Area: 76,639 square miles; Rank: 15th
Number of Counties: 93
Highest Point: Panorama Point: 5,424 feet
Coastline: 0 miles
Inland Water: 711 square miles
Bordering States: Colorado, Iowa, Kansas, Missouri, South Dakota, Wyoming

NEVADA

Nicknames: The Silver State, Sagebrush State or Battle Born State
Statehood: October 31, 1864
Population: 1,680,900; Rank: 37th
Capital: Carson City
Largest City: Las Vegas
Land Area: 109,895 square miles; Rank: 7th
Number of Counties: 16
Highest Point: Boundary Peak: 13,143 feet
Coastline: 0 miles
Inland Water: 667 square miles
Bordering States: Arizona, California, Idaho, Oregon, Utah

NEW HAMPSHIRE

Named after Hampshire, England, by Captain John Smith

Nickname: Granite State
Statehood: June 21, 1788
Population: 1,168,200; Rank: 42nd
Capital: Concord
Largest City: Manchester
Land Area: 8,992 square miles; Rank: 44th
Number of Counties: 10
Highest Point: Mt. Washington: 6,288 feet
Coastline: 13 miles
Inland Water: 286 square miles
Bordering States: Maine, Massachusetts, Vermont

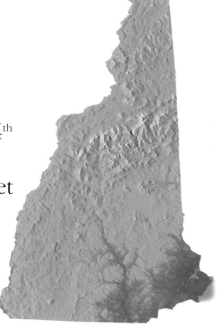

New Jersey

Nickname: Garden State
Statehood: December 18, 1787
Population: 8,015,400; Rank: 9th
Capital: Trenton
Largest City: Newark
Land Area: 7,468 square miles; Rank: 46th
Number of Counties: 21
Highest Point: High Point: 1,803 feet
Coastline: 130 miles
Inland Water: 319 square miles
Bordering States: Delaware,
New York, Pennsylvania

New Mexico

*Named by the Spanish for the
lands north of the Rio Grande River*

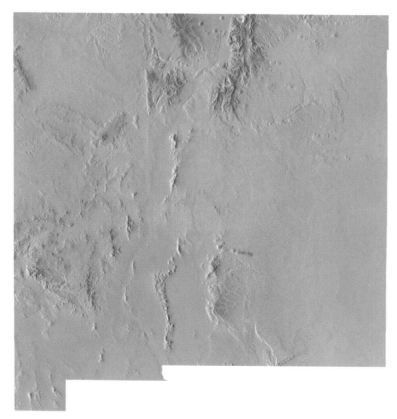

Nickname: Land of Enchantment
Statehood: January 6, 1912
Population: 1,723,800; Rank: 36th
Capital: Santa Fe
Largest City: Albuquerque
Land Area: 121,336 square miles; Rank: 5th
Number of Counties: 33
Highest Point: Wheeler Peak: 13,161 feet
Coastline: 0 miles
Inland Water: 258 square miles
Bordering States: Arizona, Colorado, Oklahoma, Texas, Utah

NEW YORK

Named after England's Duke of York

Nicknames: Empire State or Excelsior State

Statehood: July 26, 1788

Population: 18,195,400; Rank: 3rd

Capital: Albany

Largest City: New York

Land Area: 47,379 square miles; Rank: 30th

Number of Counties: 62

Highest Point: Mt. Marcy: 5,344 feet

Coastline: 127 miles

Inland Water: 1,731 square miles

Bordering States: Connecticut, Massachusetts, New Jersey, Pennsylvania, Vermont

North Carolina

Taken from "Carolus," the Latin word for
"Charles," after England's King Charles I

Nickname: Tar Heel State
Statehood: November 21, 1789
Population: 7,382,500; Rank: 11th
Capital: Raleigh
Largest City: Charlotte
Land Area: 48,843 square miles; Rank: 29th
Number of Counties: 100
Highest Point: Mt. Mitchell: 6,684 feet
Coastline: 301 miles
Inland Water: 3,826 square miles
Bordering States: Georgia, South Carolina, Tennessee, Virginia

NORTH DAKOTA

From the Sioux Indian word for "Friend"

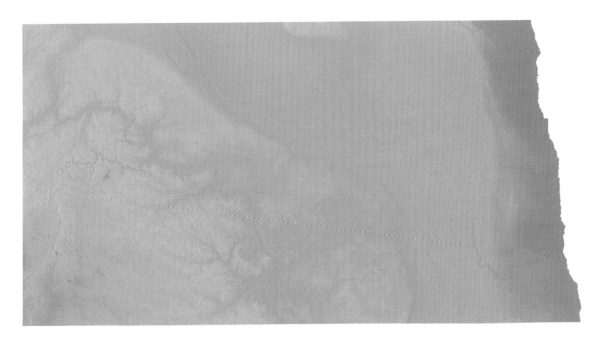

Nicknames: Peace Garden State, Flickertail State or Sioux State
Statehood: November 2, 1889
Population: 664,900; Rank: 47th
Capital: Bismarck
Largest City: Fargo
Land Area: 69,299 square miles; Rank: 17th
Number of Counties: 53
Highest Point: White Butte: 3,506 feet
Coastline: 0 miles
Inland Water: 1,403 square miles
Bordering States: Minnesota, Montana, South Dakota

OHIO

From the Iroquois Indian word meaning "Good River"

Nickname: Buckeye State
Statehood: March 1, 1803
Population: 11,201,300; Rank: 7th
Capital: Colombus
Largest City: Columbus
Land Area: 41,004 square miles; Rank: 35th
Number of Counties: 88
Highest Point: Campbell Hill: 1,550 feet
Coastline: 0 miles
Inland Water: 325 square miles
Bordering States: Indiana, Kentucky, Michigan, Pennsylvania,

OKLAHOMA

Based on Choctaw Indian words for "Red Man"

Nickname: Sooner State

Statehood: November 16, 1907

Population: 3,314,200; Rank: 27th

Capital: Oklahoma City

Largest City: Oklahoma City

Land Area: 68,656 square miles; Rank:19th

Number of Counties: 77

Highest Point: Black Mesa: 4,973 feet

Coastline: 0 miles

Inland Water: 1,301 square miles

Bordering States: Arkansas, Colorado, Kansas, Missouri, New Mexico, Texas

OREGON

Origin and meaning of name unknown; may have been derived from the name of the Wisconsin River, shown on a 1715 French map as "Ouaricon-sint"

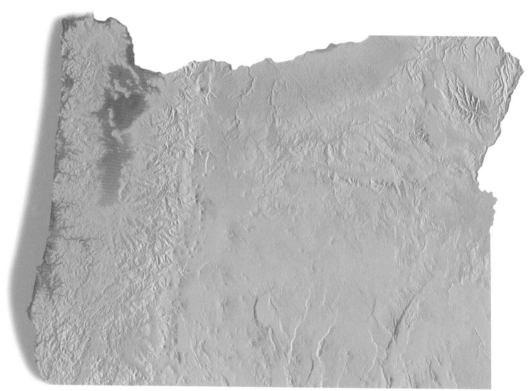

Nickname: Beaver State
Statehood: February 14, 1859
Population: 3,235,500; Rank: 29th
Capital: Salem
Largest City: Portland
Land Area: 96,187 square miles; Rank: 10th
Number of Counties: 36
Highest Point: Mt. Hood: 11,233 feet
Coastline: 296 miles
Inland Water: 889 square miles
Bordering States: California, Idaho, Nevada, Washington

PENNSYLVANIA

*Named in honor of Admiral William Penn,
father of William Penn, the state's founder*

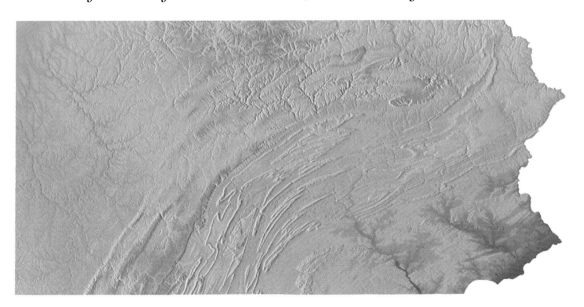

Nickname: Keystone State
Statehood: December 12, 1787
Population: 12,061,600; Rank: 5th
Capital: Harrisburg
Largest City: Philadelphia
Land Area: 44,892 square miles; Rank: 32nd
Number of Counties: 36
Highest Point: Mt. Davis: 3,213 feet
Coastline: 0 miles
Inland Water: 441 square miles
Bordering States: Delaware, Maryland, New Jersey, New York, Ohio, West Virginia

RHODE ISLAND

Possibly named in honor of the Greek island of Rhodes.

Nicknames: The Ocean State or Little Rhody
Statehood: May 29, 1790
Population: 986,200; Rank: 43rd
Capital: Providence
Largest City: Providence
Land Area: 1,054 square miles; Rank: 50th
Number of Counties: 5
Highest Point: Jerimoth Hill: 812 feet
Coastline: 40 miles
Inland Water: 158 square miles
Bordering States: Connecticut, Massachusetts

SOUTH CAROLINA

Named in honor of England's King Charles I

Nickname: Palmetto State
Statehood: May 23, 1788
Population: 3,716,400; Rank: 26th
Capital: Columbia
Largest City: Columbia
Land Area: 30,207 square miles; Rank: 40th
Number of Counties: 46
Highest Point: Sassafras Mountain: 3,560 feet
Coastline: 187 miles
Inland Water: 909 square miles
Bordering States: Georgia, North Carolina

SOUTH DAKOTA

From the Sioux Indian word for "Friend"

Nicknames: Mt. Rushmore State or Coyote State
Statehood: November 2, 1889
Population: 734,800; Rank: 45th
Capital: Pierre
Largest City: Sioux Falls
Land Area: 75,956 square miles; Rank: 16th
Number of Counties: 67
Highest Point: Harney Peak: 7,242 feet
Coastline: 0 miles
Inland Water: 1,164 square miles
Bordering States: Iowa, Minnesota, Montana, Nebraska, North Dakota, Wyoming

TENNESSEE

Named after Cherokee Indian villages called "Tanasi"

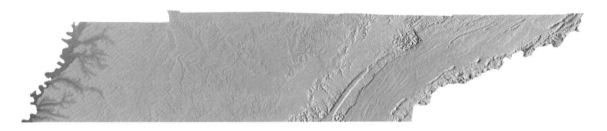

Nickname: Volunteer State
Statehood: June 1, 1796
Population: 5,342,200; Rank: 17th
Capital: Nashville
Largest City: Memphis
Land Area: 41,154 square miles; Rank: 34th
Number of Counties: 95
Highest Point: Clingman's Dome: 6,643 feet
Coastline: 0 miles
Inland Water: 989 square miles
Bordering States: Alabama, Arkansas, Georgia, Kentucky, Mississippi, Missouri, North Carolina, Virginia

TEXAS

Based on the Caddo Indian word meaning "Friends"

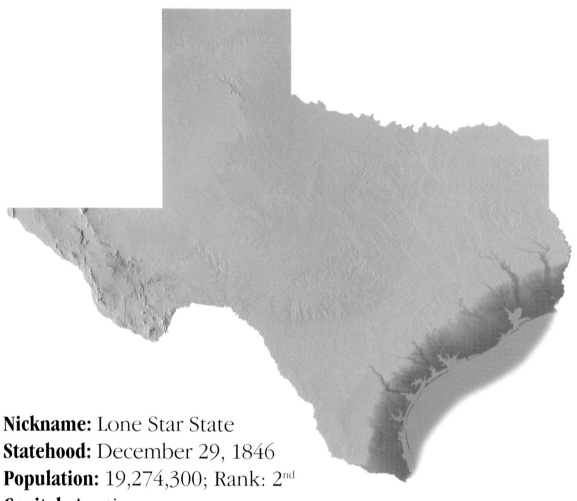

Nickname: Lone Star State
Statehood: December 29, 1846
Population: 19,274,300; Rank: 2nd
Capital: Austin
Largest City: Houston
Land Area: 262,015 square miles; Rank: 2nd
Number of Counties: 254
Highest Point: Guadalupe Peak: 8,749 feet
Coastline: 367 miles
Inland Water: 4,790 square miles
Bordering States: Arkansas, Louisiana, New Mexico, Oklahoma

UTAH

Taken from the name of the Ute Indians, whose name means "People of the Mountains"

Nickname: Beehive State
Statehood: January 4, 1896
Population: 2,030,200; Rank: 34th
Capital: Salt Lake City
Largest City: Salt Lake City
Land Area: 82,076 square miles; Rank: 12th
Number of Counties: 29
Highest Point: King's Peak: 13,528 feet
Coastline: 0 miles
Inland Water: 2,826 square miles
Bordering States: Arizona, Colorado, Idaho, Nevada, New Mexico, Wyoming

VERMONT

Based on "Verts Monts," French for "Green Mountains"

Nickname: Green Mountain State
Statehood: March 4, 1791
Population: 590,600; Rank: 49th
Capital: Montpelier
Largest City: Burlington
Land Area: 9,273 square miles; Rank: 43rd
Number of Counties: 14
Highest Point: Mt. Mansfield: 4,393 feet
Coastline: 0 miles
Inland Water: 341 square miles
Bordering States: Massachusetts, New Hampshire, New York

VIRGINIA

Named for England's "Virgin Queen," Elizabeth I

Nickname: The Old Dominion State

Statehood: June 25, 1788

Population: 6,709,100; Rank: 12th

Capital: Richmond

Largest City: Virginia Beach

Land Area: 39,700 square miles; Rank: 37th

Number of Counties: 95

Highest Point: Mt. Rogers: 5,729 feet

Coastline: 112 miles

Inland Water: 1,063 square miles

Bordering States: Kentucky, Maryland, North Carolina, Tennessee, West Virginia

WASHINGTON

Named after George Washington

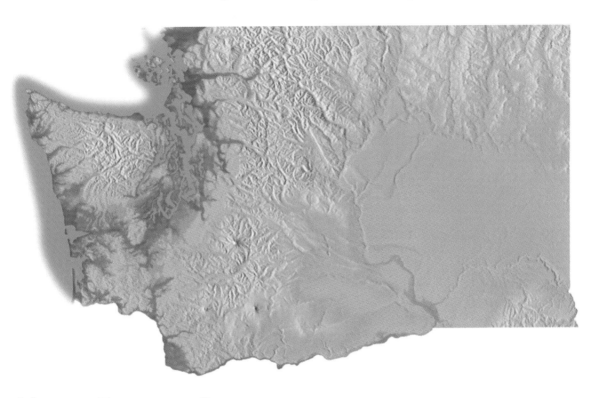

Nickname: Evergreen State
Statehood: November 11, 1889
Population: 5,590,400; Rank: 15th
Capital: Olympia
Largest City: Seattle
Land Area: 66,512 square miles; Rank: 20th
Number of Counties: 39
Highest Point: Mt. Rainier: 14,410 feet
Coastline: 157 miles
Inland Water: 1,627 square miles
Bordering States: Idaho, Oregon

WEST VIRGINIA

*Like Virginia, named after England's
Queen Elizabeth I, the "Virgin Queen"*

Nickname: Mountain State
Statehood: June 20, 1863
Population: 1,826,700; Rank: 35th
Capital: Charleston
Largest City: Charleston
Land Area: 24,124 square miles; Rank: 41st
Number of Counties: 55
Highest Point: Spruce Knob: 4,863 feet
Coastline: 0 miles
Inland Water: 112 square miles
Bordering States: Kentucky, Maryland, Ohio, Pennsylvania,
Virginia

WISCONSIN

Based on the Indian word "Ouisconsin," believed to mean "Grassy Place" in the Chippewa tongue

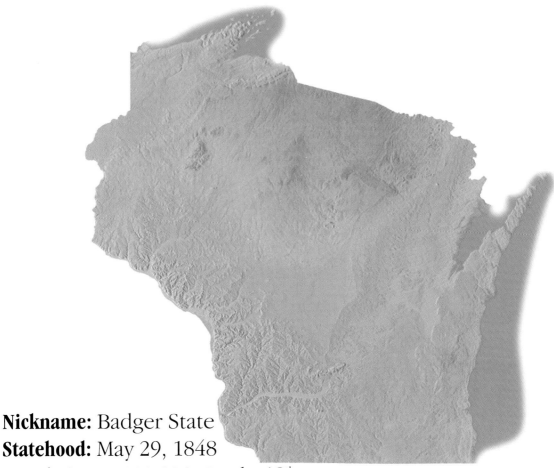

Nickname: Badger State
Statehood: May 29, 1848
Population: 5,180,900; Rank: 18th
Capital: Madison
Largest City: Milwaukee
Land Area: 54,424 square miles; Rank: 25th
Number of Counties: 72
Highest Point: Timm's Hill: 1,952 feet
Coastline: 0 miles
Inland Water: 1,727 square miles
Bordering States: Illinois, Iowa, Michigan, Minnesota

WYOMING

*Based on an Algonquin or Delaware Indian
word meaning "Large Prairie Place"*

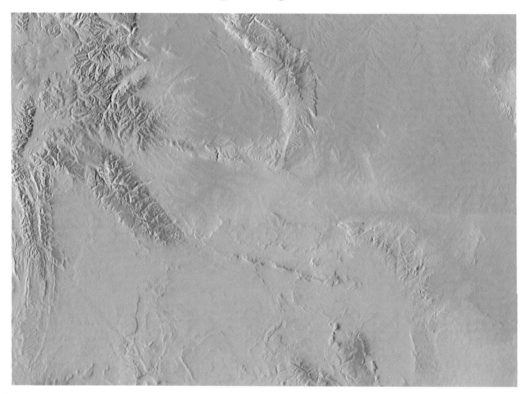

Nicknames: Equality State or Cowboy State
Statehood: July 10, 1890
Population: 482,400; Rank: 50th
Capital: Cheyenne
Largest City: Cheyenne
Land Area: 96,988 square miles; Rank: 9th
Number of Counties: 23
Highest Point: Gannett Peak: 13,804 feet
Coastline: 0 miles
Inland Water: 820 square miles
Bordering States: Colorado, Idaho, Montana, Nebraska,
South Dakota, Utah